Of Darkness and Light

*Penned poetry and prose,
beings solid and those not seen.
From the Vampire to Angels
and of this life in-between*

Lisa Herman-Gagnon

Writers Club Press
San Jose New York Lincoln Shanghai

Of Darkness and Light

All Rights Reserved © 2000 by Lisa Herman-Gagnon

No part of this book may be reproduced or transmitted in any form or by any means, graphic, electronic, or mechanical, including photocopying, recording, taping, or by any information storage or retrieval system, without the permission in writing from the publisher.

Published by Writers Club Press
an imprint of iUniverse.com, Inc.

For information address:
iUniverse.com, Inc.
620 North 48th Street
Suite 201
Lincoln, NE 68504-3467
www.iuniverse.com

ISBN: 0-595-00216-1

Printed in the United States of America

I wish to dedicate this book to my family
who are my roots and strength.
I love you all so much!
To my dearest friends, my source of energy,
inspiration, and hope.

But most of all,
to my beloved husband Bill.
Thank you for your unconditional love,
never-ending support
and unwavering faith and trust.
To love eternal, always.

Darkness and Light

What is darkness
but the absence of light,
and what is day
without a night.
What is sorrow
but joy removed,
and what is love
without the truth?
What is knowledge
but the absence of fear.
And what is evil
but goodness not near.
What is positive
but a negative reversed,
and what is humanity
but the self preserved.
What is insanity
but a memory lost,
and what is clarity
but absence of thought?
What is life
but certainty of death.
And when he comes,
what is left?

Darkness

To the shadows that linger
just out of sight.
To the cries that echo
out into the night.
To the darkness that calls
to one and all,
Listen, but be careful
do not fall.

Dreamwitch
1993

She calls you to her mystical world,
full of half-dreams and waking sleep.
Of bright lights cast in shadows,
of songs sung over screams.
Realities laced with illusions,
fantasy based on fact.
In that twilight time when she clouds your mind
and you float wieghtlessly down to the black.
She caresses you with her fingertips,
your flesh feverish where she touched.
Kissing your wrist with soft, moist lips.
Soothing the bite with her tongue.
You cry out to control your emotions,
to hold back the desire she feeds.
You awake screaming out to the darkness,
never knowing the dream witch was me.

Amandas Tale
1993

My beloved came
on wings black as night,
eyes ablaze like fire.
My beloved gave
to me a kiss,
igniting my desires.
My beloved took
my heart, my soul,
he took my mortal breath.
My beloved gave me
eternal life,
and then my beloved left.

Darkness.Named
12-27-99

Tis not for the lonely night to speak
of those that dwell in the dark.
Tis not for the rising sun to seek
the horrors of those left marked.
Tis not for the pure of heart to know
of the evil that lurks within.
Tis not for visions of goodness to taste
the blackness of our sins.
Tis not for children's peaceful dreams
to see this terror in the night
Tis not for shy young maidens to know
the eternity of our plight.
Oh and yet we feed on those very ones
fair maiden, sweet child, tis the same.
We live in darkness eternal
the good fearful to whisper our name.

And yet we exist
Darkness named us
Vampire.

Time is near
5/16/98

The time is coming.
We want to turn away,
hide our faces and crawl into a hole
where we think we will be safe.
If we can't see, hear, touch, smell, or taste it,
it can't hurt us.
It doesn't exist.
If science doesn't acknowledge it,
religions deny it,
your neighbor disbelieves,
then it can't be true, it can't happen.
If your teachers don't teach you,
your friends don't understand,
and your family has never experienced it,
then it can't be.
But you feel it.
You sense it deep inside,
like a worm crawling in the pit of your stomach.
Twisting and turning.
Waiting for the right moment.
You know, beyond a certainty,
that it will come to pass.
You want to wish it away,
pray to whoever or whatever will listen.
But it's still there, waiting in the shadows.
How you plead for it to cease,

to change it's course.
But it can't.
It has to complete it's mission.
And even though it will bring pain and sadness,
it will also bring great peace and love.
But, we must go through hell
to get to heaven.
Or though they say.
The time is near.

Fear

Fear
in the shadows of man's heart,
terror
of it ending before it starts.
Hungry
for emotions to feed the fire,
crying
as the soul begins to die.

Trying only to understand
the driving force behind the man.
But as it has been through out history,
if you cut a person, they will bleed.

Seeing
children playing in the light,
hearing
children crying in the night.
Knowing
what is wrong from right,
confused
when nothings left in sight.

Fear.

The Vampires Tale
10-95

The night has come with the hunger.
Like the winters I am dead and cold.
My red eyes shine,
I take to the night skies,
on wings the color of coal.

The night comes, I slowly awaken.
With the hunger, a burning need.
I give you a kiss,
with icy lips,
and drink deeply as you bleed.

To you, I am a dream lover,
Caressing you softly in the dark.
With trembling hands,
you do my commands.
Leaving you lifeless as I depart.

But with the night must follow the morning,
bringing sunlight and all that is pure.
To my crypt I then fly,
to sleep and to hide,
till the night sets me free once more…

Unforgiven
11-16-99

It's so cold…
his slender body shakes
as Decembers icy fingers
grasp him in a numbing embrace.
The freezing winds
caress his jaw line
his face so pale from the touch.
His lips tremble, split and bleeding,
the taste of his blood, bitter-sweet
like the forces of nature
that surround him.
With tormented eyes
he gazes out to the winter ocean.
A melancholy horizon
washed in shades of gray,
a palette of colors
that mirror his own life.
The spray of the ocean
caress him in a gentle mist.
The salty scent, stinging his wounds
and his memories.
The turbulent surf
crashes against the jagged cliffs at his feet,
pounding like a frantic heartbeat,
calling to him, beckoning.
Howling winds carry a song

a whispering promise of no more pain
no more suffering.
Decembers symphony of winters fury
build to a shattering crescendo.
The unforgiven
opening his arms wide
surrenders to her magical spell,
falling into the waiting embrace
of his watery lover.
And there is no more pain
no more suffering.
In a single breath…
all is gone.

When Love Dies...
12-27-98

So this is what it's like when love dies,
one left confused, another to cry.
So this is what it's like to give too much,
one left strong, the other used up.
So this is what it's like to loose your heart,
one continues on, the other torn apart.
So this is what it's like to condemn your soul,
one turns away, one left alone.
So this is what it's like to loose your mind,
one seeks comfort, the other runs to hide.
So this is what it's like to dance in the dark,
one drinks deeply, one left marked.
So this is what it's like to loose a best friend,
one finds replacements, the others hope ends.
So this is what it's like when love decays,
one carries on, the other fades away...

Anticipation

Just a glimpse.
A wispy specter,
playing among the shadows.
I hope.

Just a scent.
A pungent fragrance
carried upon a warm evening breeze.
I want.

Just a touch.
The briefest contact,
like a feather brushed over my skin.
I need.

Just a taste.
A single, precious drop,
like sweet wine placed on the tip of my tongue.
I hunger.

Just a heartbeat.
A pulsing rhythm,
like a drumbeat fading in the night.
I wait.

Flesh and Fantasy

Flesh and fantasy,
where does one end and the
other begin?
Can you have both
without risking your very soul?
Is there such a thing
as playing it safe when you
tamper with the fires of fantasy?
Fire burns flesh, this much
I know for I have been
burned before.
You think it would be easy
to control something as
simple as the flesh.
But when the mind takes over
and the fantasies start,
what then?
Are we able to pull in
the reins before it gets out
of hand?
For if you let the misty
visions of the mind run free,
you will loose control.
Then the black void will
swallow you whole.
How do you fight it?
When the body burns for the

want, the physical needs that
feed the fires.
And if the fantasy is the
fuel for that fire, you
are hopelessly lost…
But then again,
what a ride!

Forbidden
9-7-99

So this is forbidden, I care not.
Your eyes tell of lust, that I want.
My heartbeat quickens, I fear not.
Your hand reaches out, and I touch.

In darkened room, a candles light
Your hand slowly wanders, it feels right.
My breath catches, your eyes bright.
You whisper my name, swallowed by night.

Flesh against flesh, it consumes.
Stifled moans, fill the room.
Bodies entwined, ecstasy looms.
Passions race, by light of moon.

So this is forbidden, I care not
Embraced in nights arms, what we want.
Heartbeat fades, we fear not
For in the light of day, all is gone…

Dark Angel
1993

Come fly my love
on nights black wings,
come blend with the mist
by the shore.
Come run through the forest
on padded feet,
come feed on those gathered
at sleeps door.
Come take my hand
as I rise from the grave,
come dance under
the pale moonlight.
Come sleep by my side
as the sun slowly rises,
come live in my eternal night.

She
5/22/94

She rises, empty blackness.
Takes flight on dark wings.
Listen…

She hunts without mercy.
Be they peasant or king.
Listen…

She smiles, seductively sweet.
Full lips stained red with blood.
Listen…

She observes, eyes lit with fire.
Tracing circles high above.
Listen…

She touches, like wispy smoke.
A dream and yet, hot flesh.
Listen…

She consumes, hungry passion.
You cannot resist.
Listen…

She leaves you, cold and lifeless.
A smile upon your lips.
She…

Request
1-7-99

To take the darkness was my choice,
empathic spirit, inner voice.
Blindly loving, wisdom suppressed,
all I asked was a simple request.

Daylight turned to very long nights,
all the intimacies hidden from sight.
Heart divided, pulled and stretched,
all I asked was a simple request.

Happy moments began to change
being in love just wasn't the same.
You turned elsewhere, seeking your quest,
taking no responsibility for the simple request.

Alone I was abandoned with darkness and guilt,
no help from you to remove the heartache built.
To bleed it away was all that was left,
for you would not fulfill my simple request.

The simple request was for time,
time to dispel the darkness.

Shadow
9-20-99

And the shadow smiled.
his dead eyes shining cold as emerald ice.
A small chuckle escaping his blood stained lips
as he watched her die.
Oh she did it so slowly,
so beautifully.
He could hear her heart breaking
like so much fragile glass
shattering into a thousand pieces.
Each fragment a razor,
cutting at her innocent soul,
slicing away at her mortality
her morality, her blind trust.
Oh how his excitement grew!
And when the tiny spark that was
the angel, flickered out,
he breathed in deeply of her death.
Savoring his conquest.
Without a thought or word, no feeling,
no remorse, the shadow took flight.
On to find another victim of purity.

Prison
12-22-98

In one shared moment,
lives drastically change.
A soft whisper of encouragement,
turns to frustrated screams.
Shining hopes for the future,
to tortured dreams.
In one moment,
the souls stripped bare.
Uncertainty of tomorrow,
shackling hearts,
all that was given,
now tears apart.

It will take more than one moment to repair.
Alone, two separates must serve their sentences,
both confused, stumbling, struggling for repentance.
And when that moment comes, and they emerge,
will they be whole? Will they feel purged?
For just one moment can drastically change.

But if there is love, something good must remain.

Embrace

The single, silver tear,
rolls down alabaster skin.
Sorrow encased in it's liquid spirit.
No life left, he is alone in empty darkness.
A tender kiss he lays
upon her pale cheek,
then lifting up on immortal wings
off to love another.
He will leave them too,
cradled in the arms of sweet death.
An embrace he will never know.

Lady
11-2-99

The lady emerges
from dreams of passion foretold,
through the misty shadows
of midnight she strolls.
Ruby eyes ablaze from lust fed fires,
as black raven circles
and watches from high.
Crowning cascades of coal black hair,
billowing gently
in nights perfumed air.
She whispers your name
from moistened lips,
and steals your soul
with just one kiss.
You love her willingly
as your life she takes,
and die from the ecstasy
of her eternal embrace.

Beast Within
12-03-98

He is a vortex.
A black vacuum
engulfing everything that comes within reach.

He is a wall.
Hard, solid, impenetrable.
Leaving twisted destruction when you come in contact.

He is a rock.
Heavy, heartless, emotionless.
He hits with deadly force, but feels nothing.

He is darkness.
All encompassing, blinding, frightening.

He is there, within you.
Waiting, lurking, growing.

He is a part of you…forever.

Viper
10-93

When you least expect it,
when the sun is shining bright,
in the shadows of the tall grass,
is when the viper strikes.

When your life is warm and beautiful,
when your joys are many,
he slithers quietly up behind you,
and strikes without warning.

His looks are so deceiving,
his eyes a fathomless hue.
But bite is cold and deadly,
his poison quickly destroys you.
He plays at being harmless,
as he coils around your heart,
and before you know it,
he drags you down to the dark.

So when the viper visits,
don't be fooled by his harmless looks.
For when he draws back and strikes you,
you'll never get back what he took.

The Hunger
3-29-99

Out in sunlight, open and free
under blue sky, two souls seek.
A word, a glance, a whisper, a laugh,
wandering together, watching time pass.
Comes the hunger

In moments shared, nothing held back
in desperate moments, two souls connect.
A silence, a cry, a heartache, a tear,
a total surrender, no doubt or fear.
The hunger is near.

In darkened room, hidden away
by candle light two beings play.
A look, a smile, a touch, a sigh,
a kiss on the wrist, a brush of thigh.
The hunger is here.

In harsh reality, nothing remains,
all is forsaken, two decay.
No thought, no desire, no memories to heed,
no remnants of love, no desperate need.
Gone is the hunger.

Fallen Angel
8-17-93

She came with the morning sun
with gifts of love, purity and hope.
She embraced you in her arms
and you were safe.
She gave sweet music with her laughter,
and tried her best to dry your tears.
But she let the sun set.
With it came the night.
Not knowing what had happened,
she let darkness replace the light.
Her hope turned to fear,
her purity to need,
and her arms began to suffocate
the one she meant to please.

She crossed that sacred line.

Now eyes once filled with laughter,
cascade rivers of tears down her face.
Her wings now broken and shattered,
for the angel has fallen from grace.
No one will weep for her.
She alone must wear her shame.
This fallen angel.

Demon

Where do you run to
when the darkness comes,
no longer protected
by the healing sun?

Who do you call upon
to lend you a hand,
when no one will listen,
no one understands?

What is your dark secret,
the monster you hide
with imaginary stories,
distorted words and lies?

When will you realize
time is up, it's too late?
The icy crypt closes,
sealing your fate.

Why do you struggle,
why do you fight?
Give into the demon,
become one with the night.

Mistress Moon
9-7-99

You come to me and set me free,
unlocking the chains of sunlight's mortality.
Now briefly I can be what I desire to be.
Oh mistress moon, my sister.

You give me knowledge of what man keeps at bay,
to the shadows I wander where truth can lay.
Be it vibrant life or somber grave.
Oh mistress moon, my sister.

You let me experience what daylight hides
in my peaceful slumber, desires arise.
There I can view my lovers eyes.
Oh mistress moon, my sister.

In unconscious dreams I see that which is real,
things that waking day conceals.
In this time unhindered, I can truly feel.
Oh mistress moon, my sister.

I thank you.

Wolf
10-93

I would rather have a limb torn from my body,
than to be suffocated by the never-ending pain.
The black, never-ending wrenching of my heart
as it ceases to feel.
The torrential flood of tears
that spill on to the abandoned,
jagged cliffs of my soul.
All in the name of what?
This wolf in sheep's clothing,
this hell masquerading as love.

Suffer the Children
12-28-99

Chilly fall morning, hidden in shadows
a muffled cry is heard, the sound so faint,
like the wail of a dying dove.
A litter strewn alley amidst rotting garbage,
wrapped in a tattered blanket,
an infant is found.
Pale face looks up, stained with tears
and dirt. Tiny body trembling from
the cold. Her cries call for warmth,
her little arms grasping for comfort.
Strong arms reach out with a life-saving
embrace, she is swept away
to sanctuary, to safety.
She is bathed with tender care,
warm food nourishes her fragile body.
Lullabies and love chase the fear away.
Soon, a new family, a new life
filled with love and hope.

Alone in a roach infested, barren apartment,
no food, no heat, no hope.
Curled up fetal on an old stained box-spring,
a young child-mother lies in the dark,
bleeding from open wrists, a broken heart.
She dies alone and cold,
a plea of forgiveness on her lips.
Forgiveness from her God, and her child,
both she had abandoned.
She herself, thirteen years old.
Suffer the children.

The Program
7-3-99

The insanity,
this constant gnawing uncertainty called life.
We walk around balancing shadow and light,
sometimes confused with eyes wide open.
We reach out to society and ask,
"Now what?"
Oh, you must deny that intricate part of who you are,
because we know what is good for you,
what is best, forget the rest.
Be responsible,
the good boy/girl, the good employee,
the good father/mother, the good husband/wife.
Now isn't this better?
Now you can be content, happy, fulfilled.
The insanity is still there, so we ask,
"But what about."
Oh, there is nothing else.
Forget passion, forget the desires, forget honest dreams.
Forget anything that made you feel good.
Let us dull you with pills, programs, preaching.
Now don't you feel better?
Your a good boy/girl, your normal, now you fit right in.
But uncertainty gnaws so we ask,
"But who am I?"
Oh you are what we want you to be.
Devoid of originality, cleansed of that part of you

we don't want to see.
You are now perfect.
Dependable,
programmable,
with eyes wide shut.

Drink to Life

Let's drink to life
and all it will bring.
To the times that we've wept,
and the times we shall sing!

Wisdom

Adult petty differences are problems of their own making.
I do not care about them.
They have lived enough years to know right from wrong,
existed long enough to formulate their own opinions and views.
I have no respect however,
for the adult who lets a child suffer because of it.
If people have differences and come to harsh words over it, so be it.
But keep it away from the child's ears.
And if you need distance from the other individual, then take it.
But do not isolate the child.
Do not neglect them or let them feel any blame.
But go to them for peace.
You can learn great things from them.

Through a child you can find innocence
and purity of the heart once more.

Angel '99

A fall evening.

A ray of light
pierces the darkness
slicing through engulfing shadows
like a sword,
aflame with knowledge and truth.
Burning with wisdom and strength
born of justice and love,
shining gold as the color of her hair.
And they called her purity.
And in her eyes
Heavens peace and tranquillity
are given freely to those who hunger.
In those liquid pools of ocean blue
hope shines forth.
And in her arms
the lonely and frightened are safe,
given freely to all who want.
Her gentle and soothing embrace
giving love and comfort.
And under her wings
the color of billowing summer clouds
there is shelter.
Calm from life's raging storms,
protection from the unseen shadows,
given freely to all who need.

And in her voice
comes the beautiful music of truth.
Like a gentle breeze whispering,
soothing your beast, your unspoken fears.
Given freely to all who seek it
for what is fear but the lack of truth.

Then deception came calling
masquerading as a seeker of truth and love
that even the Angel was blinded.
Now, with a single tear
one shimmering silver drop of precious hope lost
she is gone.
Now, she will fight to heal
for Angels too can bleed.
But she will return
and justice and truth will prevail
Hope, wisdom, strength and love
will be the Angels gifts once more…

Will You Be There
7-93

Will you be here at my side, my love,
though I give you cause to doubt.
Will you be there when I loose my way,
will you be there to guide me out?
Will you be with me when I play in the sun,
though I sometimes forget you are there.
Will you be there to protect me when it rains,
will you be there to show you care?
Will you be there when I speak my mind,
though the words might cause you pain.
Will you be there to encourage me on,
will you be there all the same?
Will you be there when I hurt inside,
though the pain may not be for you.
Will you be there to comfort my broken heart,
will you be there to help me through?
Will you be there when my final breath I take,
though you know it will leave you alone.
Will you stay by my side, my husband, my life,
be forever my soul mate,
my beloved, my home.

Hero Child
9/7/98

With tiny hands and large heart,
the first born son makes his way alone.
Armed with wisdom learned through trial by fire,
a heavy burden for one so young.
Kind spirit, keen intuition, love and happiness,
begin to fade with age.
For the hero child knows only to give,
loosing himself along the way.
Years of pain, rivers of tears and blood,
a caring heart that starts to break,
for the young warrior, lover and teacher within,
slowly begins to fade.
Bruised and dazed from the battle raged,
his mind spinning out of control,
frightened by another side of himself,
he never wanted to know.
Left stumbling at the gates of hell,
in search of the child that died,
he finally reaches up and takes the hands,
of the few who never left his side
Now strong enough to ask for help,
realizing he's not alone.
Wrapped safely inside the wings of love,
the hero child has finally come home.

I Will Wait
5/1/98

Sometimes you speak in riddles, endless circles.
Like a carnival ride that leaves you dazed and disoriented.
Even though it stops where it started and reveals little,
still I listen.
You make plans with absolute certainty.
And like a whirlwind, I'm caught up in the vortex.
Even though they never materialize,
still I wait.
You do your best to distance yourself from me.
Like a child playing hide and seek.
Even though you remain visible with words,
still I'm patient.
I must be.
I believe a small part of you would like to see me turn away.
Give up and not waste my energy.
You feel that that is the only way to exist with me,
only through disappointment.
But I see through you.
I know what's going on in there.
And I can respond the only way I know how.
I will continue to listen.
I will continue to wait.
And even if you don't believe it,
I can be very patient.
So play in the shadows,
and surround yourself with those like yourself.

If it is safe, if it's what you need.
I will wait.
I, will play in the sun.
I will tempt you out of the shadows.
I will surround you with love,
and I'll be patient.
I will listen for your call,
and you will come to me and play in the light.
Until then,
I will listen, I'll be patient, and I will wait...

Mirrors to the Soul
4-4-98

They say the eyes are the mirrors to the soul.
By looking into them,
the true essence of a person is left uncovered
and cannot hide.
All that the individual has experienced in their life,
from love, heartache, joy and despair,
reside in those orbs.
All that has been seen,
good and bad,
are rooted in the pools of color.
Every thought and action since their creation,
pure or not,
is left standing naked without disguise,
for the observer to be witness to.
I must look into your eyes.
I need to understand what is dwelling within the flesh.
Don't be afraid.
I know it can be frightening
to have someone strip down
the layers of armor that have been protecting you.
To have another soul reach in,
embracing the very essence of who you are,
taking it gently into their hands
so you can be discovered and understood.
It's so much easier to look away and hide.
So much more comfortable to keep the walls around you,

your darker side protected from the pain
that can be associated with laying open the soul.
But remember,
to every time there is a season.
And for every little death,
there is a glorious birth.
And for every soul,
there is a kindred spirit waiting...

Being Enough?
11-99

Why can't being, just be enough?
Why must some be attracted
to mirrors of themselves?
Turbulent pasts to turbulent pasts?
Why must light be feared, neglected, rejected?
Why is it assumed
that some are "too good"
or "deserving of better"?
I, for one, grow tired of the label.
Don't tell me what's best for me.
Don't tell me I deserve better.
Don't make up my mind for me!
I will not apologize
because my childhood was sweet.
I will not apologize
because my life has been good.
I will not apologize
for being who I am,
surrounded by those who love.
You can either accept it,
share and be a part of it,
even though I have nothing in common
with your tormented past,

or go back to what you know.
Those who share familiar fears with you.
But do not choose for me!
Why can't being, just be enough?

Breathe

Breathe deep
the scent of skin,
breathe deep
of the fragrance within.
Breathe deep
the perfumed night,
breathe deep
now gone from sight.
Breathe deep
a choking laugh,
breathe deep
your sorrow masked.
Breathe deep
the shuddering sigh,
breathe deep
as you silently cry.
Breathe deep
of memories past,
breathe deep
love too good to last.

The Wall
3-13-98

You surrounded yourself with an impenetrable wall,
locking yourself within its cold, dark womb.
I approached,
beating at it until my hands are bruised and bloodied,
every muscle aching.
But you would not let me in.
So I reluctantly stepped back,
trying to find a peaceful place within myself
where I could observe, unattached, and wait.
You fought your demons in the bowels of your fortress,
and I waited.
When the battle was over, you emerged triumphant.
But in the course of tearing the wall down,
I took a step forward and became trapped by the falling debris.
Stone by heavy stone, I'm buried alive by it's crushing weight.
Years and years of disappointment, lies, hopelessness and fear,
buried within it's granite mass,
pushing the life out of me with each hit.
I wish I could be there to see you shine,
But I've gotten too close
and someone had to pay the price.

Battle for the Soul
3-6-99

To be a spiritual warrior,
incarcerated in perfect flesh.
You are judges by outward appearances,
not by inward kindness.

Oh young man, awkward being,
struggling with wrong and right.
At war with human wickedness,
with mankind's moral plight.

You've judged yourself too harshly,
forsaken what you loved most.
In honesty, there is purity,
now haunted by memories ghost.

To seek perfection of the spirit,
to forgive yourself and learn to just be,
rest the body, calm your thoughts,
now let the soul run free

Escape

You hid away, the bruises will fade,
the painful words, the fear.
"No little sister, this is not right!"
I grip the phone, my knuckles white.
"But he loves me" she whispers,
her voice small in my ears.
While I, a continent away,
can only imagine her fear.
"It's not that bad" she tries to convince,
Oh but I know otherwise.
Her red hair torn from her scalp
bruised ribs, bloodied mouth.
The mental picture fills my mind,
the blinding rage,
tears fill my eyes.
"Oh God, little sister, why keep silent?
How could you not let us know!"
"But he said he's sorry, he said he loves me,
that it won't happen again"
Tears trail down my cheeks,
"Until the next time sister,
tomorrow, next week?"
"Run little sister, take your babies and fly,
come be with your family, it's safe you can hide."
"But I love him" she whispers
and silently cries.
My anguish engulfs as I try to console.

"No little sister, this is not love,"
I wipe at my tears, feeling her do the same
though she is not near.
"Love does not use, does not abuse,
does not hit with fists and demeaning words.
Making you feel less than nothing,
till you believe the same.
Love does not leave you bloodied and bruised,
hurting in body and heart"
"I know" she cries, her pain fills me.
"Come home little sister, to love, to healing,
to those who would never hurt, only love"
She hangs up the phone,
takes her children and leaves,
joining her family,
Setting herself free.

Kindred
3-10-99

To see you laugh, makes my spirit take wing and fly,
to see you hurt, causes my heart to silently cry.
We Kindred

To watch you succeed, makes my soul celebrate!
But when your heart bleeds, mine desperately aches.
We Kindred

When I see your small victories, my voice rises to sing!
But to observe your destruction, my being screams.
We Kindred

You have let me touch your heart, I respond in kind.
You give to me your pain, and excepted mine.

Sunlight and Shadows
1-7-99

You dwell in the shadows, it's where you are comfortable.
I played in the sunlight, it was all I knew.
Then one day our paths crossed.
You stood in the shade of a large oak tree, sunglasses on.
Our eyes met, we connected.
"Find your peace," I whisper as we parted.
You walked away, but not out of my life.

Days turned into months,
and the times that I do see you, it's at night.
Your form lingering in the smoky shadows of a bar.
Months turn to years.
I continue to live in the light,
but I find my vision drifting to the shadows.
Hoping to get a glimpse of you.
My thoughts returning to you, wishing you happiness.

Then the day arrives. We meet again.
Though parted for years, it seems like no time has passed.
You though, have fallen too far into the darkness.
Your eyes haunted by memories of love lost,
your soul tortured as you fight to find yourself.
All I can do is let you know you are loved.
That I am here for you.
But you had to fight the demon alone.
So I waited.

New year comes, calls of attempted self-destruction.
Of nightmares made realities by addictions.
I am here, let me help you please. Shared tears and fears.
My eyesight now locked to the shadows.
I don't dare look away. I must keep my eyes on you.
I cannot loose you, will not loose you.
I stand on the edge of light and shadows.
Then I step over, arms outstretched to you.
To join with you, to help, to guide you towards the light.
And you do cross over, very briefly, and you smile.
But in visiting the shadows, I threw the balance off and I fell.

Now, we are back where we started.
I in the sunlight, healing. You in the shadows, healing.
Though not together, but watching each other from afar.
Forever kindred spirits that shared a unique love.
Both changed, both wiser for the experience.
Both stronger in different ways for what was exchanged,
in that place between sunlight and shadows.
^o^

Whisper
'96/update-1999

One can see
that you are very passionate
about your opinions and ideas,
as we all are at times.
That can be healthy.
But I must warn you to be careful.
Be careful
that they do not cross the line
into obsession.
Or even worse,
fanaticism.
Rage is blinding,
and anger,
just one letter short
to danger.
Teach with tolerance and understanding,
love and compassion.
Remember,
Empires have fallen,

with just a whisper.

War

Mankind's spirituality
has failed to keep pace with technology.
Therefor, we are left stumbling in the fog
of our own intelligence.
The mind and the soul working against each other
instead of hand in hand, as one.
And with such a battle, no one wins.

God help us all…

Wolf Song
1-09-2000

He stands so still, contemplating.
Deep brown eyes focused.
The winter air rustles his thick coat.
Raising his head, he sniffs,
the scent of something catching his attention.
And still, he does not move.
Lowering his head he continues to stare.
A flash of pink tongue as he licks his jaw,
a flash of sharp fangs.
He starts to pace, right, left, then back again.
His eyes locked on something,
those deep eyes filled with…
with what? A human quality,
a knowing presence?
He stops his pacing and stand still once again.
The only movement, the whiffs of breath
in the cold air surrounding him.
And yet his stare calls me out.
I stand, mirror to him.
Blue eyes locked to brown,
matching breath for breath.

Yes, I know what it is I see
standing behind the cage.
Kindred souls, both human, both animal,
both creatures of God.
He lifts his head, sending out a mournful cry,
and my heart breaks in understanding.
Now I realize, we both, in our own ways,
are lost in our own prisons.

Can I Be There
7-98

Can I be there when you need me,
can I answer when you call?
Can I offer my arms to hold you,
when your emotions start to fall.
Can I give you what you want,
can I heal you when you hurt?
Can I make your pain go away,
when your feeling so unsure?
I wish that I could give you
the answers you want to hear.
But the truth is I'm uncertain,
I'm afraid when you get near.
It's not that I can't love you.
I can and would like to try.
But I shake when I try to hold you,
and it causes me to cry.
So now I'm left just wondering,
where do we go from here?
Do I take that blind leap of faith,
to prove I hold you dear?
Now, it's a two way street,
and I can't give without receiving.
It's not that way with everyone,
but with you, I must protect my feelings.
In order for my soul to survive

and not vanish in a dark empty space,
you must be willing to give part of yourself,
we must see face to face.
I wish that I could give you,
the answers that you seek.
But alone I am not strong enough.
Alone, I am too weak.
So please don't judge me too harshly,
or be disappointed by my faults.
Believe me when I wish you love,
and will care deeply, no matter the cost.

Noise
3-23-98

I'm tired of your voice.
Prose and poetry that make no sense.
Words that confuse and distort.
I think you enjoy hearing yourself talk,
even though you really have nothing to say.
Mindless chatter,
empty words like black caves.
They tempt and draw you in,
but leave you stumbling blindly in the dark.
It's a noise that echoes off the walls,
giving a false reading of where we are.
And when we step forward, bam!
We hit a hard, cold stone wall.
I'm tired of the never ending, cascading waterfall
of sayings and verse.
Your not as cleaver as you believe yourself to be.
Can you just be quiet?
Can you silence your ranting and raving for just a second?
I'm deaf from your ruckus.
Please, give me peace and quiet.
Let me wrap myself in blissful silence.
Something you should try.
Then maybe your soul will have a chance to breathe.
For once, let there be peace…

Soul Survival
2-2-99

To be so close,
yet standing alone.
Souls forever united,
never to share a home.

To be joined together,
yet exist apart.
Sharing of spirit,
but not of heart.

To be so close in thought,
yet physically miles away.
Living out today's reality,
remembering yesterday.

To the souls survival,
the memories prey.
The heart sheltered by a purer love,
until the memories fade away.

Street Soul
1-94

Don't look at me with pity,
don't judge me with disgust.
I did not ask to be here,
it's just been my bad luck.

You'll cross the road to avoid me,
ignore me as you walk quickly by.
You seem to forget I am human,
that there is pain inside these eyes.

You'll stop to pet a stray dog or cat,
for one moment give it love.
But if I try to talk to you,
you push by me with a shove.

You've chosen to give me many names,
street person, bag lady, bum.
But my life was once like yours,
I didn't know this tragedy would come.

So as you go home to your loved ones,
your shelter, your family and food.
Remember the next time you pass me,
that tomorrow this could be you.

Innocent Lost
12-98

A gun goes off, a life is lost
oh dear God what have we done?
A small hand trembles
as the smoke clears
a child stands alone, an innocent lost.
A lifetime so short, an eternity of fear
oh dear God how can this be?
No tears fill the eyes
no regret, no cries,
a child stripped of humanity.
Locked in a cage, labeled insane,
oh dear God who is to blame?
What thing has done this,
please give us a name
but silence is the only reply.
A gun goes off, a life is lost
Oh dear God please tell us why?
A child abused,
beaten and used,
innocent lost said a final goodbye.

Ties That Bind
2-16-1998

It makes me wonder,
when I call you on the phone,
hope to hear your voice, but no one's home.
I wonder.

Do I question,
past conversations and words you said.
Were they from the heart? Or from the head?
I question.

I feel the pain within your chest,
I see the scars upon your wrists.
And for every teardrop that you cry,
adds another strand to the ties that bind.

I understand,
that the roads we travel are the ones we choose,
and this one I walk, I walk with you.
Do you understand?

I believe,
that your friendship gives me treasures untold,
ones to cherish, ones to hold.
Believe me.

And I feel the pain within your chest,
and I see the scars upon your wrists.
And for every teardrop that you cry,
adds another strand to the ties that bind.

To D.E.L, the scars and the ties.

Moment in Time
10-93

For a moment in time,
I want to see with your eyes,
feel with your heart,
think with your mind.
Too tired to keep guessing,
hurts too much to try,
I ask myself the same question,
ask myself why.
For a second or two,
I want to feel your tears burn,
hurt with your heart,
see what you've learned.
I just want a small glimpse
of the person inside.
Then I will truly see you,
you won't be able to hide.
But the reality is I can't,
so I must see on my own,
feel with my heart,
trust what I am shown.
So we will keep the masks on,
play out the charade,
as the walls build around us,
dying a little each day.

Caught in the Web
11-98

There was a time, not so long ago,
when I could gaze into the eyes of a friend.
But time flies by and I question why,
that time is at an end.
We turn on the machine, click on a button,
talk to the world through cyber space.
Their voices we can't hear, their eyes we can't see,
the monitor replacing the face.
Welcome to the computer age,
of e-mails and chat rooms galore.
Mankind has moved forward, embraced the machine,
can't remember what it was like before.
It's a double edged sword we must reluctantly accept,
in order to stay in touch.
But I can't help but sigh at days gone by,
when we could look in to the eyes of love.
So let's remember fondly the days of old,
and think warmly of cherished ones.
Then turn off the machine and get up from the chair,
go out and play with a friend in the sun…

Swan Song

You were the breath,
that gave me speech.
You were the song,
my heart longed to sing.
Your eyes held the vision
that gave life to my dreams.
Your desire and passion,
warming fire for my being.
Your lips spoke of promises
carried inside shared hearts.
Your arms a sanctuary,
giving comfort from the dark.
But time became the messenger
that separated two to one.
Kindred rent asunder
to truly know love.
Your thoughts are the hope
of the future to come.
Your spirit the reason
my soul will go on.

The Gentle Heart
2-7-99

Is love by some, so easily forgot?
Not by this,
the gentle heart.

Are soft spoken words that were whispered, not truth?
Not by some,
though maybe for few.

Is the brush of lips for only lust to take?
Not for this,
not for the spirits sake.

Are the years spent caring, all for naught?
Maybe for some,
but for few, 'tis not.

Is friendship so easily cast away?
Maybe for the shadows,
but not for the brave.

Choices
9-3-99

The gift.
The ability to choose.
Right from wrong,
those we wish to share our lives with
and those we can not.
How we love,
the chances we take,
the paths we walk down.
The gift.
Choices.
Good and bad,
prices that must be paid,
situations that can't be ignored.
The gift.
A clear head
a calm soul
a heart at peace.
or
A haunted history
a tormented spirit
a heart that ceases to feel.
The gift,
Choices.

Hate
10-93

The greatest sorrow of mankind
is that this word came into existence.
If we do not abolish it soon,
it shall ultimately be our destruction.
And the terrible shame is
the wound would have been self-inflicted.

The Challenge

I have no time
for friendships of convenience.
Like simple banter
it is wasted energy
and lifeless breath.
Let me taste of your soul
then my friend you shall be.

You Went Away
9-16-99

It was six years ago you came my way,
we lived each moment, savoring each day,
bound forever by kindred ways,
I never imagined you would go away.

You asked for my heart, I gave what I could.
You tasted my soul, and smiled, it was good,
You embraced my body as I knew you would,
and still you went away.

Why was what I gave freely, not enough?
Why did you take it all and run?
Why did you abandon a friend you loved?
How could you go away?

It was not long ago I heard your cries,
and I was there, I stood by your side,
and when it came my turn to cry,
you turned and ran away.

Days turn to months, months to years,
we live without each other, because of your fears,
so we sadly give up what we once held dear,
all because you went away.

Separtion
9-25-99

For this moment,
this space of time in our lives
we must sacrifice our time with each other.
Nights when you must sleep alone,
and days when I do the same.
Take my thoughts of pure love,
wrap them around yourself as you lay to rest.
Let them lull you into blissful slumber,
dreams filled of the two of us together.
Smiling, laughing, sharing, loving.
During the few days I must be without you
I sleep on your side of the bed.
Holding your pillow close,
breathing in the scent of you.
It does not take the longing away,
but it comforts, it soothes, it will do.
Our life together is so much more precious
more priceless, our love, absolute.
I never thought I could love you any deeper
but with these moments of separation, I do.
In love we are and shall forever be.
So let's look to the near future that is coming,
when we will never have to be apart,
when we will never have to sleep alone.

Now kiss me, my love
as you go off to work,
and I lay down to sleep with the rising sun.
It will not be long, I promise.

Father Time.
12-21-99

For some your hands move too slowly
forever taking their time,
and I thought it true
as I pushed through my youth
eager to leave my childhood behind.
Now for others you move at break-neck speed
leaving them grabbing for life on the fly
but these are the ones
whose youth have gone
and they can't seem to bid it goodbye.
I have noticed with the coming of age
(and yes, we pass through many)
you leave wisdom each time
a knowing certainty of mind
with a fathers guidance, turn our pages.
So Father Time, I thank you
as I grow in both darkness and light
the precious time you give
so we may truly live
knowing eventually it will all turn out right.

Let There Be Light

And to the light
which guides us all,
may we embrace it with love,
when it comes to call.

Apart
8-28-93

Arthur's Seat, Scotland

As I stand upon this hill,
where Kings walked
and battles raged,
where lives were lost
and loves proclaimed,
I feel the cool wind
and gaze at all horizons.
Though body and soul are here,
my heart lies elsewhere.
With you my husband, my love,
in a far off distant land

A Childs Eyes
1-94

When you look into a child's eyes,
you can see such splendors there.
Little men and unicorns,
playing everywhere.
But only in a child's eyes.

Look into a child's dreams,
lovely princesses with golden hair,
tiny fairies with sparkling wings,
flying here and there.
But only in a child's dreams.

But as we grow, we loose the child,
the innocence and purity of soul.
The lands of peace and fantasy,
suddenly become barren and cold.
Shattered by man's realities.

Oh how I wish that I could see
the way the child now views me.
To have it back what time has wrought,
to be so pure in heart and thought.
I wish…

If you look into a child's soul,
see the innocence so pure.
The unspoiled loveliness,
a feeling so warm and secure.
So look into a child's soul.

Let There Be Light

We have been searching so long,
for what seems like an eternity.
The illusions of many lifetimes passing us by.
Night go on forever, casting shadows
in the recesses of our souls, roaming the dark
corridors of the heart for that ever elusive light.
We travel down memories of the minds eye,
indistinguishable shapes washed in shades of gray,
nothing defined, no vibrant colors.
We seek vainly with eyes not accustomed
to such darkness, tripping over non-existent barriers,
walking into stone walls of our own making.
We try desperately to find a way out of the endless maze.
We listen with ears cocooned in silence,
desperate to hear the song of the soul,
the melodic rhythm of the heart.
Are we dying?
Then a saying, just a few perfect words come through.
They are blasted upon us with such force,
pushing us back to the world of color, beauty and light.
Such a warm light!
It surrounds us with laughter, music and love.
We turn to thank our savior,
and find ourselves gazing upon our own reflection.
Smiling, there is a soft whisper echoing in our hearts.
"Let there be light."

Night Music

Be still. Don't speak, just listen.
There is so much music to be heard,
but only in silence.
The song of a nightingale
as it greets the gentle evening breeze.
The cricket and toad
harmonizing over the buzz of insects
in a marshy swamp.
The hum of fireflies
that light up the darkness
in a fairy tale display.
The hoot of the owl
as it listens for the rustle
of a mouse in the tall grass.

All beautiful music.

But in order to truly hear and appreciate it,
you must be silent.
Calm your busy thoughts.
Don't let them spill forth
in mindless chatter.

Just listen…

Keepers Call

Stormy evening of Dec. 6,1999.
Heceta Head Lighthouse

Aye, the ocean is angry today
the winds howling like a lover scorned.
The waves, pounding against the rocky cliffs below
like an angry, petulant child.
Oh! But the night comes
with her blanket of velvet darkness.
And the beacon of the guardian shine forth,
blazing like shafts of white hope.
Tis safety my lighthouse gives.
Tis comfort and warmth she promises.
And we, weary travelers,
are always welcome.

Stirrings
4-8-98

A feeling stirs from within,
like a butterfly emerging from a cocoon.

The sensation grows,
just like the creature with gossamer wings,
that takes flight towards the healing rays of the sun.
I know from where the stirrings come,
a kindred spirit, a person I love.

You, like the butterfly,
have awaken from the dormant darkness
that held you for so long
wrapped in silent oblivion.
And I watch daily with admiration as you,
little by little, brake free from your prison,
to spread your wings to the warm light.
And the feelings grow stronger.

I, too, know what it is like to
be blanketed in hopeless oblivion.
Like yourself, I broke free,
embracing the light of love and hope.

The thoughts you send, I receive,
and the moments we spend together, are precious.
The feeling are with me daily,
a picture of you carried in my heart.

And many times,
I send my light in your direction,
and revel in the waves of happiness
that float back to me.

We are creatures of a soaring spirit,
momentarily dwelling in a house of flesh.
It is our souls that will always be connected.
And when the flesh is gone, we will not
cease to have the stirrings.
They will only be stronger and all-encompassing
as we become part of that bright light.

So, until that time comes,
I will treasure the stirrings I have for you within,
and I will joyously hold you in my arms
and be content with what we share.
It is a rare thing, these stirrings.
These blessed emotions of the heart.
But most of all, it is shared.

Squeeky

This morning, I said goodbye to my friend,
a companion, a child.
Sixteen years, sixteen.
You were placed in my hands just a tiny little thing.
A throwaway, tossed in a garbage can.
People can be so soulless.
Your little meows cried out for warmth,
food, most of all, love.
Sixteen, it's so hard to believe.
Your days of playing with your wacky wall walker,
chasing a laser beam across the floor with the speed
of a younger cat, amazing those around you.
You have seen more of the world than most people.
Never complaining, never questioning, never doubting.
In my darkest time, when no one was around, you stood vigil.
My guardian, my protector.
Giving me love, unconditionally.
Oh if we humans could learn to be that way.
You started your life in the palms of my hands,
and you died curled up in my arms.
I couldn't have asked for more.
Like the sun that shone brightly this morning,
you have given me sunshine, brightened my life.
It is fitting that you should leave this world in sunlight.
Thank you, for being in my life. I will miss you so.
This morning, I said goodbye to my friend.

Squeeky. 1983–1999

Old Souls
11-2-99

Your youth, I do not seek,
although it makes me smile.
So young, and yet I see
in strange young eyes, familiar tears.
Rich brown eyes tinged by similar fears.
I, with my years of lessons learned,
older, and yet, not much wiser.
You, soulful eyes,
have traveled a rough road for one so young.
Where I, a friend,
walked a more sheltered one.
And yet, we are both old souls.
You, with your youth,
I, with my experience,
find balance in each others company.
Finding friendship in trust.
You, with your past hardships,
I, with a past pain still healing,
are able to share a trust born from old souls.
Sharing freely of friendship and joy.
Where, in it's simplicity,
purity and honor,
kindness and caring,
are once again,
for the old souls,
gained...

For my friend Jason, I thank you for your trust.

Sun Child

In a time before this present reality, this life,
in an age of innocence and purity.
I knew of a sweet, golden hair child who
loved to sing and dance among the clouds.
So young and full of grace,
her only need to share her sweet smile and laughter.
In the dew of the morning, she would frolic
in fields of rainbow colored flowers that
danced in the breeze around her.
Her melodic songs lifted up to the wind and
mingled with the sounds of nature,
creating a beautiful, hypnotic music that
could calm the fiercest beast.
At noontide, she would run along the soft golden sands.
Her laughter, tinkling like bells,
would blend with the rhythm of the ocean.
Her eyes, sparkling as blue as the sea, her
song of joy carried on the waves that danced at her feet.
The sun envious of her bright light.
And if the skies were cold and gray,
she would dance circles in the falling rain
as it gently showered her with drops of liquid silver
Her song, once again, rising above the blowing winds.
The Gods applauding with claps of thunder
for she is truly a child of their making.
In the peaceful silence of a starlit sky,
under the dark blanket of night,

she hums softly a lullaby as the world sleeps.
It carried you on gentle wings,
to a simpler, peaceful time.
As I drift into slumber, I run to greet her,
I go to embrace innocence.

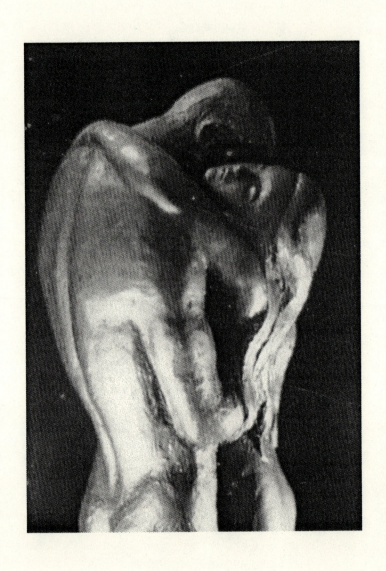

Heaven
2-9-99

In the peaceful silence of the night,
by the glow of golden firelight.
Two separate hearts beat in time,
legs, arms, bodies entwined.
The brush of your lips across my breasts,
passionate kisses that steal my breath.
Your body that covers in a warm embrace,
in perfect rhythm with mine, as passions race.
Hands move tenderly, caressing your face,
my mouth seeking out yours, to savor, to taste.
Blue eyes locked to mine in kind,
sending the gift, telling me you are mine.
Two souls sharing a pure love such as this,
bodies finally exploding in faultless bliss.
Now with my head resting upon your chest,
Cocooned in perfect contentment,
we finally rest.

Sisters

My sisters,
oh my sisters.
What a life we share.
Our hopes, our dreams, our promises,
with ones we know who care.

My sisters,
yes my sisters.
It's crazy but it's true.
My life would not have been this great,
if it had not been for you.

True, when we were younger,
we did quite often fight.
But then the words, "I'm sorry",
made everything all right.
And as we grew,
we went our ways,
but always kept in touch.
For being apart of each others lives,
always meant so much.

So a toast to you my sisters,
and I hope you are doing fine.
Please know my love for each of you,
will last throughout all time.

Mom

She is light and love.
She is warmth and joy.
Her words, soft and kind.
Her hands gently guiding.
She chases away the fears,
always drying my tears.
Always understanding,
a sympathetic ear.
She listens without judging.
She is the essence of love itself.
Endlessly giving
to all the children that surround her.
Oh to be so selfless,
I can only gaze in awe.
To be like her
would be so wonderful!
I will always give thanks
and love you, Mom.

Dad

For my Father.
With careful hands and gentle words,
you tended your seedlings, your children.
And like the gardener,
that nurtured the fragile buds,
you can now celebrate the vibrant oasis
that has emerged around you.
Precious life.

Happy birthday Daddy,
Love daughter number one.

Child

I heard a sound carried on the wind,
I knew not from where it came.
It seemed to emanate from all around,
slowly driving me insane.
I turned around and stumble upon,
a child crying in the cold.
Her sobbing spoke of a thousand pains,
the deaths of a thousand souls.
In a single tear I saw mankind,
the damage we had wrought.
The destruction of the planet,
the wars that we had fought.
In her pain filled, amber eyes,
I saw children dying alone.
No food to fill their stomachs,
no shelter to call their home.
As the wind began to calm,
and sunshine parted the clouds.
A rainbow washed over her body,
erasing her face of the frown.
She looked up to the deep blue sky
and gave me the sweetest smile.
And there, I saw the hopes of tomorrow,
shining brightly in her eyes.

As she left, she touched my hand,
in my palm lay a single tear.
And as she slowly faded away,
there was only hope, no fear.

Sometimes
10-13-92

Sometimes,
I think of how nice it would have been if we could feel
things the same way.
Not loosing ourselves, but experiencing a touch
without holding hands or physical contact.

Sometimes,
to share the same dreams without using our eyes,
but to see them with a deeper vision.

Sometimes,
to sing and hear the same song, but without the use of voices or ears.
Instead to share the song with the breath of our hearts and souls.

But sometimes,
the feelings, the touch, the dreams and the song, are too different.
And the distance between two souls, too great.

So sometimes,
when we meet my friend,
I shall be content to physically hold your hand,
speak to you of my dreams,
and sing to you a different song.

Slumber
5-2-99

Sitting on the couch, legs pulled up, head resting on my knees,
I watch you peacefully sleep.
My blues eyes resting on your beautiful face,
I wonder with a small smile,

"What do you dream about?"

Do you soar above cities, gliding without wings?
Do you see yourself in concert, thousands mesmerized as you sing.
Do you participate in games of chivalry, a knight on a field?
Or maybe a wizard creating magic with the wand that you wield.
Do you live in a magnificent castle, nestled deep in a forest green?
Or in a lighthouse perched atop a cliff that is beaten by stormy seas.
Are you visited by your parents who bring comfort in the night?
There bodies no longer with us, their souls part of the light.
Are you building your guitars, to share the gift of music with man?
People from across the globe wanting to share in your plan.
Are you helping the less fortunate that are lost in desperate plight?
But this is something you already do, in your waking life.

I get up from my comfortable contemplation and kneel at your side,
laying a tender kiss on your forehead.
I do not know what you dream, my love.
But no matter which one of these scenarios
is playing out in your slumber,
I hope I am with you in all of them.

The Stage
1/24/99

On a dimly lit stage,
a figure emerges.
One form standing alone,
one man who hurts.

As the lights go up,
he is joined by another.
One who has been there,
one who has suffered.

Kindred spirits,
linked in kind.
Both searching for peace,
both hoping to find.

Hand in hand,
they speak of the past.
Of hopes that were shattered,
loves that couldn't last.

The lights start to dim,
they go separate ways.
Each remembering the new friend,
they met on the stage.

to Eric Z. Kind friend, generous spiritr...
I thank you...

Teach Me
7-93

Teach me,
for you know so much of this world where I am blind.
Like a child stumbling in the darkness.

Teach me,
for I want to learn of this place, this time.
Like an innocent I know nothing.

Teach me,
help me to understand all these others that surround me.
For I feel so alone in this crowd.

Teach me,
how not to fear the strangers, the shadows, the thoughts.
For I am sometimes left confused.

Teach me,
of this thing called love, help me to understand the soaring heart.
I know I have wings but have yet to fly.

Teach me,
I trust you to always be gentle and kind.
Please, all I ask is for you to teach me.

Lay Me Down

Lay me down in pastures green,
under a canopy of blue skies,
let the birds sing sweet melodies,
as they dance with the clouds up high.
Give me a halo of flowers gold
to wear upon my head,
let their fragrances perfume the air,
as we lay down in natures bed.
Let the cool winds caress our skin
as we passionately embrace,
let the warmth of the sun melt our garments away,
as I tenderly kiss your face.
Let passions flow like wild winds through our souls,
like raging rivers empty into the sea.
Not only uniting two bodies as one,
but two hearts in ecstasy.
Lay me down in pastures green
as the cloak of twilight falls,
and under a sky of diamonds bright,
let's give again to loves passionate call.

Pray
12-93

As you lay your head down to sleep,
say a prayer for me.
For you I will do the same.

When you wake with the morning,
say a prayer for me.
For you, I will do the same.

And when your life gets to be too much to bear,
say a prayer for me and know I'm there.

When you see something beautiful,
say a prayer for me.
For you, I will do the same.

As you gaze up to the heavens,
say a prayer for me.
For you, I will do the same.

When this life is over and your time is through,
I will be the angel, and the first to greet you.

In loving memory of Barbara Phillips.

Love
5-93

How can one word have so many meanings?
Is it the word itself,
or mans inability to explain the unexplainable?
To properly define that which has confused mankind
since the beginning of time.
To give this word a substance,
a physical body that we can touch and feel and say,
"This is love."
For some people believe in only what they can touch.
Others shall explain this word only as a feeling.
A sensation that can only be expresses
by the soul.
A thing that does not need words or physical contact.
Something with no definition.
A soaring feeling shared by the purest of hearts.
To me, love is all of these things.
For me, love needs no definition.
For me, may love just always be,
indefinitely, eternally, forever…

The Wish

I wish.

For a chance to mend the chain,
for lost friendship to be found again.
For absent love to be revealed,
for broken trusts to be healed.
For peaceful moments when two were one,
for scars of punishment to be gone.
For a heart that questions to be at peace,
for the power to change what has been.
To remove the doubts and guilt of love,
to re-discover a friend that is gone.
But I have learned as precious time goes by,
some wishes can never be,
but at least I tried.

Soul Mates

The connection was made by the sound of your voice.
Though I could not see you, I felt my heart open wide.
Then I saw your face, and in your blue eyes, there was love.
I got the honor to know you as a best friend,
and from that grew true love.
You have given me the best and scariest times of my life.
You gave me the gift of music, and held my hand when times were hard.
Never questioning or setting boundaries,
you gave me the most precious gift of all.
The freedom to live and learn. To grow and succeed
and reach for my dreams.
And when some of them came crashing around me,
leaving me heartbroken, you were always there to help me back up,
to hold me, telling me that you love me.
What is love?
It is the time we spend laughing and singing,
arguing and making up again.
It is trying news things together,
and returning to what is always comfortable
and constant. Our love for each other.
It is sharing joys and sorrows,
life and death, and knowing that we will never be alone.
So many things I could tell you, so many things I can list,
that it would be a never ending tale of what you mean to me.

Only one word is needed, one simple word that says it all.
Every emotion, every experience, every dream,
and you have given it all to me.
Love.

Anger

Don't be so angry
little man,
for the way your life's turned out,
don't blame society
little man
for the chaos that's come about.
Don't be so bitter
little man,
for the injustices that you see,
don't blame the green God dollar
little man
not everyone lives for greed.
Don't lash out blindly
little man,
because things appear so twisted
Don't speak so coldly
little man,
not everyone's lives are wasted.
Don't be so hurtful
little man,
because your child inside is lost
Don't be so angry
little man
because of your choices and their cost.
Don't blame society,
don't blame your childhood,
don't blame the money

don't blame the bosses
don't blame the system.
You made the choices,
you take responsibility.

The children know truth,
it is adults that teach them otherwise.
Don't be so angry,
little man.

Hate is hate.
No matter how you package or preach it.

Hope
1/6/99

Shattered Man.
Slumped behind a Plexiglas wall.
Phone in hand, eyes cast down.
I never imagined you would fall,
so far, so hard.
I sat across, but cannot touch.
So I whisper in the receiver,
speak of love, of hope.
Please look at me, my beloved friend.
You glance up, locking eyes with me.
The walls crumble without and within.
The incarceration is now shared.
We trade hopes and despair, wants and fears.
Sharing uncertainty of tomorrow
and all it will bring.
All is said without words for they are not needed.
We place our hand against the glass,
wishing it was gone.
And even though its there and solid,
we know with certainty we will survive.
We must.
There is so much more to come.
Hope.
We grab at it, wrap it around our hearts.
And now, months later.
You are strong and free to choose,

what will come, what will be.
The shattered man gone forever.
Our lives have changed,
though hearts still entwined.
The future, now on course.
The past tinged with some remorse.
But hope will always survive.
And we, my beloved friend,
shall be always together,
though forever apart.

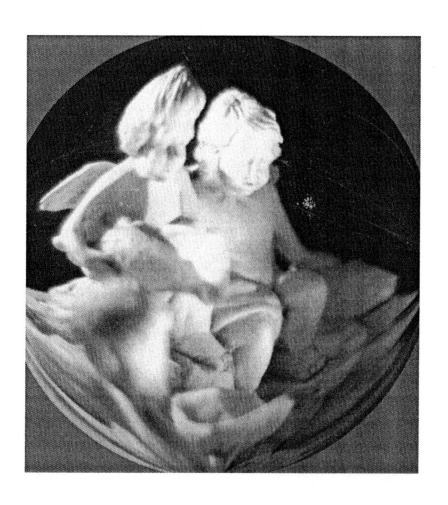

Give Thanks

Smile, not only on your lips, but in your heart.
Give thanks for another year of living and learning.
Of laughter and tears, love and disappointments.
All that which helps us to grow without, and within.
Give thanks for being able to smell the perfume of a rose.
To see the flaming orange colors of a setting sun.
To hear the music of the wind through the trees.
To feel the rain as it softly falls upon your face.
To breathe deep of the crisp clean air after a summer storm.
To run barefoot through the tall grass
and dip your toes into a cool stream.
Give thanks for being able to reach out
and touch the hand of a friend.
To see the smile of a child, hear the sweet laughter.
To know the comfort and love in a single embrace.
To feel the wind caressing your hair,
the sun warming your skin.
The gift to gaze up into a midnight sky
and watch the shining stars dance!
Give thanks for tears and pain felt, for in doing so
you give vibrant life to the smiles, laughter
and love of memories past! And with it, comes peace.
For this time is precious and brief.
Remember and give thanks.

Wings
2-2-99

Oh for a pair of wing to fly,
above the pain, above the strife.
Far from the suffering, all the tears,
all the destruction, all the fear.

Oh for a pair of wings to soar,
away from stupidity, far from the wars.
Away from heartache and the guilt,
the concrete barriers that man has built.

Oh for a pair of wings to glide,
above the earth, wrapped in clear blue skies.
Over crystal oceans, clean and bright,
during midnight hours, peaceful night.

Oh for a pair of wings
so that I may seek,
that which is good in humanity,
the pure in me.

My White Knight
10-9-99

I awaken with the magic of the dawn,
the music of the lark,
the perfume of the rain.
My White Knights arms wrapped around me,
your tender touch, slow, rhythmic breathing of sleep,
soothing like a gentle caress.
Trying not to disturb your slumber,
I position myself so I can gaze into your peaceful face.
Oh my White Knight! My husband and mate.
How blessed am I!
Unable to resist touching your beauty,
I brush my fingertips lightly across your cheek
and you stir.
Opening your sapphire blue eyes,
you smile.
Like a rose, lifting it's petals to the warming sun,
my lips slightly part as you lean in,
tenderly kissing my waiting mouth.
Once again, fulfilling every want, every desire
with abounding love.

~My White Knight, I am eternally yours~

Printed in the United States
1694